ACCEPTING CHILDREN UNCONDITIONALLY

HOW TO SUPPORT, UNDERSTAND & LOVE YOUR CHILD

PREETI MEHROTRA

ISBN 979-888555144-1

Dedicated to my daughter, who encouraged me to accomplish something wonderful for which she may be proud.

Contents

Foreword

From guilt to acceptance and the struggles in between. A wonderful portrayal of what parent's experience while raising children with differences and unique abilities.

Preeti takes us through a journey of doubt, diagnosis and hope, in a world of cookie-cut-out students, she recounts with her vast teaching experience that raising a child who won't fit the mould.

She explains with real-life examples that living with children with behavioural issues and a slow processing Speed deficit can make you feel like you're in a constant battle with your brain.

She guides parents that every day, you have to reassure yourself and stay in control, to not screw up--forget living up to your potential. But in her book, she gives clarity that what you might not know about, and what's even more damaging, is the constant, corrosive emotional stress of a lifetime spent wondering what the hell is wrong with you and your child.

Preeti in her book helps readers identify, manage and address issues with practical, proven advice including understanding the link between Slow processing Speed and emotional distress. What emotional turmoil parents and family members go through and how to create an emotionally safe place for such children.

She has provided many tools and guidelines to help parents go through such difficult situations and move past the pain and shame towards a future full of possibility, acceptance, balance and joy.

It is a beautiful portrayal of the journey - from guilt to acceptance and the struggles in between...A practical experience of what parent's experience while raising children with differences.

Ramaa Shankar
Success Enabler,
Career Coach &Web Designer

Testimonials

If you wish to envisage a perpetually youthful face with a constant smile. Preeti. Preeti was a classmate of mine. She has always been a responsible person with a strong desire to attain her goals. Preeti has grown up from a lively girl to a responsible mother and devoted wife. She has always been a nice friend with whom you can discuss your thoughts and receive practical counsel. Now that she has put this gift of hers into words (a book), I wish her all the best in her future endeavour.

Ashish Trivedi
Area Sales Manager
Patanjali

It's been almost ten years to known a woman in person, whose charismatic personality came across in our very first meeting. Confidence, extremely hard working and tenacity is inevitable. Yet so calm and encouraging to her colleagues is what makes her the woman she is - Preeti Mehrotra. I, with full conviction, can profess that Mrs Preeti is one of the most ambitious, consistent at same time humble people I've encountered in my life.

Harsha Pamnani
Intern in Child counselling (DUBAI)

Preeti is result driven and brings vast teaching experience to the fore when it comes to guiding youngsters to choose the best fit careers. She is a career coach who works persistently to help students realize their dreams. She has taken her passion to the next level and caters to all types of students from different backgrounds and age groups. She creates awareness about the importance of skills, aptitude, interest, and personality in the area of work. She is a skilled advisor providing positive direction and motivating students to follow their dreams to achieve success. One can rest assured about picking the right career path and a career roadmap for themselves after consulting with her.

Ramaa Shankar
Success Enabler,
Career Coach &Web Designer

Preeti is my close childhood friend. Having known her for more than three-quarters of my life, I have seen it all. From being a reckless neighbourhood tomboy to a fun-loving emotional teenager who grew up to become an empathetic, humble and honest human being whose positivity is almost contagious.

Her selfless, friendly disposition instantly connects with people. Embracing others without judging, makes her a trusted confidante of many. She is a repository of untold stories which has helped her mature as a person and evolve as a creative thinker.

Preeti is cherished, and I am honoured to have known her for this long. I wish her good luck in all her future endeavours.

Reeti Prabhas
Vice President
Barclays

I have known Preeti since kindergarten, she is efficient, detail-oriented and extremely competent in what she does. Preeti also has an excellent rapport with people of all ages. Her excellent communication skills allow her to connect with all kinds of people and is an inspiration to them. I wish her good luck in all her future endeavours

Ritu Arora
Consultant Pathologist

Preeti is a person who could articulate her thoughts very well. Her friendly nature and her unprejudiced attitude have helped people open up to her and share their experiences struggles and learnings. It comes as no surprise that my dear friend of childhood has blossomed into a writer. As she ventures into this path, she touches the lives of most of us as we struggle through parenting, to help us see this as a journey that is exciting, with never with a dull moment, that helps us shape up as better human beings and help our kids be one too.

Nitin Varma
Managing Director-India & SAARC

I have known Preeti for more than three decades. We were in the same school and since then she tended to help people. She was always a sounding board for most of her friends who came to her for advice on various problems which they have been facing. Now that I look back why all of us used to come to her was because she was genuinely interested. Her sensitive and caring nature made her perfectly capable of handling the situation with ease. Today, as I write this foreword to her captivating book, I share words that I always hoped—and in many ways knew—I would have the chance to write.

Vineet Grover

AGM Sales

A word of encouragement, constant support and timely guidance can make your life beautiful. Ms Preeti Mehrotra, my career counsellor made this possible in my life. Initially, I had certain doubts and queries regarding my career plans but her counselling, suggestions and personal efforts paved the way to a clear understanding and conscience towards the same. Thank you for your support and guidance.

Nidhirvyay Naman Palariya

Grade 12

I truly loved the session and got to know about my strengths and areas where I need to work on. It was a fruitful session. After the report analysis, I got to know myself better. Thanks a lot for the session

Riya Jindal

Grade 10

Choices are right, but guidance makes it perfect. After passing my 12th standard, I had certain doubts regarding the available career options as per my interests. Mrs Preeti Mehrotra helped me to manage my feelings, interest and brings clarity to my choice of career. She also assisted regarding subject selection for the graduation. Today, I have absolute clarity, clear consigned and complete assurance, all thanks to career counselling provided by Preeti Ma'am. I am thankful from the bottom of my heart to Mrs Preeti Ma'am for guiding me. I would strongly recommend having a career counsellor like Preeti Ma'am.

Thank you, Preeti Ma'am.

Ruchika Joshi

Grade 12

I was confused and frustrated after completing my school and hence I needed someone to show me the right path and proper career options as per my interests, abilities and stream. Earlier I was not knowing about career counsellors but later I learnt about the same. I contacted Preeti mam for my counselling session. She suggested to me certain details regarding my qualifications, skills and interests. She has not only helped me to explore the best career options but enhanced my confidence level too. Thank you so much Preeti mam for your guidance and support.

Mayank Pandey

Grade 12

Mrs Preeti Mehrotra my education counsellor was exemplary; the counselling session and career report were good. The report on me was very perfect; I could relate myself with every point mostly. The counsellor was clear, understanding and helpful. After the counselling session, I got to know more about career options which I can choose and a clearer vision for the next steps. The enlightening session overall... thank you, Ma'am.

Feedback by Parent's - The Career Coach, Preeti Mehrotra helped us understand the various aspects of Laksh 's personality, abilities etc. and better clarity on which streams he can select. We are very happy and satisfied with the whole session. We are glad that we did it for Laksh to understand his interests and personality better. Thank you.

Laksh Khatri
Grade 10

Preeti ma'am aided me to see a path forward to achieving my goals and beginning a new chapter in my life. Through psychometric testing, I can learn about the type of individual I am and how to deal with negative thoughts and feelings in the future. You had also encouraged me by sharing wonderful ideas, and I appreciate your assistance with my problems. Thank you very much, ma'am

Priyanshu Tripathi
Grade 12

Acknowledgements

I would want to express my heartfelt gratitude to team Arfeen & Irfaan for not only bringing my ambition of being an author a reality, as well as for assisting me in overcoming my apprehension of writing.

I'd want to recognise and thank every member of the BTF for their incredible support and participation in my book-writing adventure. Thank you to Tasnim, Colleen, Shahin, Amal, Ikram, Deepna, and Ravinder for their great recommendations.

I am grateful to my dear friends and colleagues - Ashish Trivedi, Harsha Pamnani, Ramaa Shankar, Reeti Prabhas, Ritu Arora, Nitin Varma & Vineet Grover for their testimonials and well wishes, which inspired me to finish my book. Special thanks to Rama for contributing the foreword to my book.

I am grateful for the compassion and encouragement of my Soka family members. Swati Kekre deserves respect and recognition for making me motivated & inspired.

Finally, I'd want to convey my love and thanks to my husband, Rahul, daughter Anusha, and niece Roopanshi for their assistance, support, understanding. This book would not have existed without their assistance.

Table Of Contents

Introduction

"A Lot of Parents Will Do Anything for Their Kids Except Let Them Be Themselves"

Banksy

Parenting entails raising your child to be a self-sufficient human being. To help your kid develop not just physically but also intellectually, emotionally, and socially for them to have a more successful life. This book will help you understand your child's difficulties and techniques for dealing with them.

Parenting is difficult; parents struggle with every issue, but they love their children more than anything else. That is the allure of parenting. The book shows how parents may assist their children, learn and build confidence in their daily activities by demonstrating unconditional love, care, and acceptance.

Each of us is distinct in our way. We all go at our own pace. Every day, we all deal with our day-to-day challenges and do our utmost to overcome them without letting others know how hard we are working. Children are particularly vulnerable. Perhaps the children are too young to understand this judgmental environment. Their limited understanding is bewildered by the language that various people use for them.

This book covers two major topics. SLOW PROCESSING SPEED IN CHILDREN AND WHY DO CHILDREN ACT UP." Parents are unaware of the reasons why their child struggles to complete normal tasks that other kids effortlessly do. And feel contempt, as they battle every day, from cleaning their teeth in the morning to getting them to sleep at night. Without seeing their child's hardship, parents continue to expect that they catch pace with others. The child is frequently labelled as sluggish or stubborn and chastised for not doing it on purpose, but the truth is that he cannot.

There is indeed a reason for every action. We are often taken aback by the behaviour of our children.

The book's first chapter poses the probing question: "Why is my child slow?" Through examples, the chapter explains sluggish processing speed and the reasons for it.

The second chapter addresses the topic, "Why do children misbehave?" Act Up is described, as well as why it exists.

The solutions for dealing with sluggish processing speed and acting up are covered in the third and fourth chapters.

Throughout Chapter 5, I provided my commandments, which I would observe in my life as I learned the causes of slow processing speed and behaviour problems in children.

In a nutshell, the book urges parents to see the world through their child's eyes rather than expressing and pushing their preferences and interests on the child. Parenting is all about instilling in your child the confidence to spread his or her wings and soar

CHAPTER ONE

Why my child is slow in doing things?

"It shouldn't matter how slowly a child learns as long as we are encouraging them not to stop"

Robert John Meehan

How long would you spend in the restroom? Is it because of you that I'm running late again? You can't complete a single task on time. You're useless in every way. Because of you, I've had to put up with a lot. Parul's mornings begin with her shouting over the daughter 'Sakshi'. till she realises her daughter has Processing Speed deficiencies.

Sakshi was previously thought to be lethargic, and everyone assumed she didn't care. But Parul later regrets shouting at her to get things done.

I would like to share another instance of my cousin who recently visited us.

My cousin came to visit us after a long time, so we arranged an expedition. When he heard this, he began yelling at his daughter to hurry up in a loud tone. When I questioned him why he was being so harsh, he answered it was because my daughter is sluggish in everything she does. She is, without a doubt, clever. She's curious and intelligent, but her grades are slipping as a result of her sluggishness. She does not have enough time to complete her examinations and tasks.

Her thoughts wander. She's usually soaring about in the clouds. Since she can't concentrate on her homework, it takes up the entire evening. However, concentrating is not a difficulty when reading or watching movies. She reads a lot and can sit and read for lengthy periods. She takes far too long to complete her food, take a shower, and do everything else. Her teachers are angry because the schoolwork worsens and it becomes tough for them to get her to do her work during the remedial hour.

She claims to try, but we notice no difference. It's driving us crazy. When we don't see any results, we suspect she's baiting us and we yell at her or have her mother do chores for her so she can manage her time.

When he was talking about his kid, I had a flashback to two years ago, when I was a schoolteacher at one of Bhopal's renowned schools. The school's director summoned 4-5 faculty because a new session was set to commence in a week. I was assigned to 4F and informed that these children require instructors who can educate with love and compassion. Within a month, I saw that practically all of the kids struggle with finishing their work, understanding, and submitting assignments on time, as well as having some behavioural difficulties, and it's not going to be simple for them. I was only aware of one autistic child in my class and had no notion there may be a legitimate basis for their difficulties. Though there were some improvements in all of the children as a result of affection and care, it was insufficient. It wasn't until my cousin told me about her daughter's doctor's diagnosis of Slow Processing Speed which I was able to connect with difficulties my class children were having and with their instructors since we were not aware nor educated to deal with students with such problems. So, when I became aware of the sluggish processing speed, I chose to undertake additional studies and write about it aims to spread awareness among parents, teachers, and children.

Unfortunately, my class students, Sakshi and my cousin's daughter are not alone in the world struggling with slow processing speed but there are many untold stories where children struggle to try hard to complete their day-to-day work and parent in ignorance misunderstand the child, feel themselves helpless and frustrated and often end with yelling or smacking the child without knowing the reason for it.

Many of us wonder, why Some children are born with an innate ability to move quickly. They run, talk, do school projects and undertake a variety of other activities at a rate that appears acceptable for their age. Other youngsters don't, or perhaps it would be more accurate to say they can't. These are children who may have processing speed deficiencies.

Not only this some parents overlook and assume that the child is stubborn, lazy, and does not give any heed to them. In reality, they make several attempts but are unsuccessful.

Let's understand

What is Slow processing Speed?

Slow processing speed occurs when humans require a significant amount of time to absorb, comprehend, and respond to information. The information might be visual, such as characters or numbers. It may also be audible, like spoken language.

Having a modest handling speed might provide regular obstacles at school, job, and in social situations. Younger children, for example, may struggle to master the fundamentals of reading, writing, and calculating. People of all ages may find it difficult to complete tasks quickly and correctly. They frequently struggle to recall new information

Slow processing speed has nothing to do with how brilliant people are; it simply refers to how rapidly they absorb and use knowledge. Having this issue, though, may cause a lot of worry and damage to one's self-esteem.

From the above stories, one can easily understand that why some kids struggle with completing their assignment, assessment at the same pace as other children is due to Processing Speed deficit. Children struggling with this deficit may have trouble processing direction, may experience difficulty getting started on tasks both verbal and written. They lack focus and have a very short span of concentration. They struggle with goal setting and planning skills.

A gifted child with slow processing speed

As a parent, seeing slow processing speed in a Gifted child may be perplexing. Gifted youngsters with slow processing speeds may look concentrated but not get much done. Homework can take hours. Grades may be lower than even the most reasonable expectations. Slow processing speed might also have an impact on social connections.

For example, you could see a gap in the classroom. Even if a youngster excels at higher arithmetic problems, they may struggle to keep up with timed fundamental multiplication tests, even if they get all of the answers correct. In this scenario, the difference in processing speed isn't as significant

Signs of Slow Processing Speed

It might bc really difficult to detect slow processing speed in your youngster.

Many children who prepare data eventually appear to be dissatisfied, unmotivated, and uninvolved at first.

- Slow handling speed can influence kids within the classroom, at domestic and amid exercises like sports.
- Children may appear recurring difficulties in Finishing tests within the given time
- Finishing homework in a sensible time
- Listening or taking notes when an instructor is speaking
- Reading and taking notes
- Solving straightforward math problems in their head
- Completing multi-step math issues within the apportioned time
- Doing composed ventures that require subtle elements and complex thoughts
- Keeping track of discussions

Signs of Anxiety

Anxiety affects everyone. However, for certain youngsters, it can also be the outcome of and be worsened by Slow Processing Speed and Visual Delays. When we are worried as adults, we freeze for a brief period. We aren't processing the information as quickly as we could be throughout that moment. We may take longer to respond, make judgments, or assess events.

This worry might cause a slowdown in processing speed in youngsters. Slow processing speed, on the other hand, might cause worry. They feed off of one other, but identifying which one comes on first is critical to determining the source of the learning difficulties.

Signs of Visual Development Delays

Visual development delays can masquerade as concentration challenges, anxiety, and slow processing speed, among other learning delays. Visual-motor skill issues, such as using scissors or glue, improperly copying letters or numbers, or the inability to discern between identical letters or shapes, are indicators of a visual delay, among many other activities that manifest as a learning delay.

Slow Processing Speed at different ages

Slow Processing Speed Cues in Preschool

- Has difficulty following instructions with several stages.
- It takes a long time to write their name down.
- Struggles to respond to inquiries, especially when asked over the phone
- During circle time, he frequently stares off into space.
- It takes him longer than most kids his age to learn how to utilise a sheet of paper and a pencil.

Slow processing speed Cues in Elementary school

- It takes a long time to take notes in class.
- Unable to do assignments in a decent period.
- Has difficulty understanding what is going on in crowded places (such as the playground during recess) since there are so many things going on at once.
- Can't make a rapid decision, such as what to eat for breakfast
- Has difficulty with timed assessments (such even simple things like what to eat), then hurries and makes sloppy mistakes.
- Difficulties following talks and responding to queries from friends

Slow processing speed Cues in Middle school

- When the teacher is speaking, he has difficulty taking notes.

- Struggles to keep up with fast-paced interactions, whether in person or online, and frequently misses sarcasm, jokes, and social cues.
- When presented with a large amount of information at once, he becomes overwhelmed.
- Frequently fail to complete exams in the allotted time, such as assessments with multi-step arithmetic problems.
- More time is required to answer inquiries and make judgments than appears to be necessary.
- Speaks slowly and frequently fails to find the correct phrase,
- Struggles to complete tasks on schedule

Slow processing speed Cues in High school

- Having difficulty keeping up with class lectures and taking notes
- Does not participate in class discussions.
- Struggles in subjects that need fast visual comprehensions, such as geography and biology.
- Tells stories so slowly that he loses track of the plot while telling it.
- Has terrible time management skills and is frequently late on projects.
- Long-term assignments are difficult to manage, and it is common to lose sight of critical information.
- Can't keep up with social media engagements

Diagnosis of Visual Delays or Slow Processing Speed

- If you feel your child is struggling with preparation pace, the first step is to speak with your child's teachers. Examine your impressions and worries to see whether the teacher has seen any of the same difficulties or ones you haven't noticed at home.
- Next, make an appointment with a Developmental Optometrist, who will look for formative deficits in your child's vision... becoming more widespread as a result of increased use of displays and tablets
- The exam will feature numerous tests that are not seen on a typical exam. A Vision therapy programme may be all that is needed to correct

these delays and eliminate the discomfort and vision-based processing speed difficulties.

- If the Developmental Optometrist feels that additional difficulties are interfering with your child's ability to learn, you may be directed to have them assessed to see what kind of assistance may be required.
- Recognizing, comprehending, and addressing the relationship between visual delays, anxiety, and sluggish processing speed is critical in getting your kid treatment. However, demonstrating empathy is critical in assisting them in recognising and managing their fear. Encouragingly working with them will show them that they are not alone and that you are there to help them.

Factors Contributing to Slow Processing in Children

- ### *Biological Factor*

The structure of neurons in the brain has been linked to sluggish processing speed. There is evidence that a fatty material called myelin, which insulates and improves the efficiency of impulses passed between neurons, may affect processing speed. According to this notion, having less myelin around one's neurons may slow down processing speed.

Neurotransmitters in the brain have also been linked to processing speed. Neurotransmitters are substances found in the brain that let neurons communicate with one another. There is evidence that the neurotransmitter acetylcholine has a function in boosting responsiveness to sensory input and may be a factor in slow reaction times and information processing delays.

- ### *Different Personality traits*

In the modern-day, both parents are working, therefore, it becomes a concern for parents if their child is identified with a Processing Speed deficit. The situation becomes daunting for both parent and child as it hurts the self –esteem. It is therefore important to understand that we all are unique in one way or the other and so are our personalities. If you observe every day we come across people of different personalities like – Enthusiastic, reformer, Helper, perfectionist and many more to mention.

In the book 'Bright Kids who can't keep up' children with slow processing generally fit into one of the three categories of personality chill kids, anxious kids & daydreamers

1. **Chill Kids** - for whom life moves at a slower rate and they are ok with it.

2. **Anxious Kids**- are nervous mostly, about their homework, schoolwork or keeping pace with friends and peers.

3. **Daydreamer kids** – Always preoccupied with something else in their mind.

If parents can identify the personality of their kids, then it helps them to understand their child.

During my teaching career, I come across students with varying levels of processing speed deficiency. I recall one such instance of a girl named 'Siya.' She battled greatly to replicate her work from the green board.

In the parents' teacher meeting, the mother highlighted her difficulties with other household chores.

She is a laid-back child who is fully aware of her flaws and accepts them. I usually send another student's notebook to make her do her assignment. During examinations, though, I noticed her become concerned as she observed other students handing test papers.

- ## *Different Learning abilities*

A learning difficulty is a problem with the brain's capacity to process ideas. Individuals with learning disabilities may not learn in the same way or at the same pace as their peers, and they may find specific bits of learning difficulties, such as the acquisition of relevant skills.

Every child is unique in his ways. To learn anything there is no one fixed method. What is required is to identify the different learning capabilities like visual, auditory, kinaesthetic and reading and writing based on child absorb, comprehends, process and retaining information. If a child is not exposed to these different styles of learning it may hinder its growth or lead to slow processing.

For example – In the class of 25- 30 students, every child has its level of understanding a group of students may understand through verbal instructions while another set of students may understand through trying hands on it whereas another group of students learn through the audio-visual method.

- ### *Parents' High Expectation*

Every parent wants their kids to become extraordinary and fantastic, They want them to be masters in all that they do. They love to hear all the good things about their children. But sometimes these high expectations become the reason for the struggle for their children.

And the most common mismatch is the fast parent with slow processing speed, where the parent completes their work as fast as possible and the child takes forever to complete homework. This leads to family conflicts and battling situations every day. This brings distress to the child and loses confidence in doing.

- ### *Overprotecting Parenting*

In this fast-moving world, where people have no time to pause and think and direct, the parents of processing speed deficit children feel restless. They have no time to set the clock to make the child complete their task or prepare plans. To keep pace with their work and time, parents help their slow processing deficit children by helping them in their chores. A lot of children who are pampered are known to have the problems solved for them, which is why they never learn or adapt.

- ### *Personal Factors*

Aside from the aforementioned elements, other personal aspects contribute to sluggish learning. A child may have suffered lengthy periods of sickness or non - attendance, as well as a loss of self. It has been shown that youngsters who lack self-confidence are typically sluggish learners.

Conclusion

Identifying the biological mechanisms at the base of slow processing speed is arguably the most critical step. Rather than condemning a child for going slowly, we should recognise that they are attempting to digest information effectively. This does not preclude us from assisting them in becoming a little speedier and more concentrated. Slow processing speed neurobiology advises that we explore alternative ways for individuals to fulfil their potential and decrease the aggravation they suffer as a result of slow processing speed.

A real-life scenario

Rebeca highlighted how her kid taught her the value of understanding your child's processing speed to reduce stress at home and school.

Rebeca was the type of person who set out to do things as quickly as possible as if she were running an imagined race. Her 10-year-old daughter, on the other hand, struggles with even the most basic activities. Every morning, it's a fight of wills to get out the door. Every day, they were late to wherever they were going, which made Rebecca agitated and unhappy.

Mismatches in processing speed — the time it takes a person to complete a task — caused this form of family conflict.

And, without a doubt, if you rush and your child moves like a sloth reclining in the sun, it's difficult not to shout. You will be late for appointments and workouts.

The same thing happened to Rebecca, who was irritated because she saw her daughter be lethargic and difficult. When she casually mentioned her circumstances to a doctor friend, she became aware of her daughter's sluggish cognitive speed. Rebecca sought the help of a therapist, which was quite beneficial to her. And she was confronted with the fact that her daughter's processing speed is well below average. Previously, she blamed her daughter for not listening to her and punished her with time outs and no gadgets, but the instant she became aware, she changed her tune. She finally stopped punishing her for taking longer than everyone else. She prepared ahead of time so that she would have adequate time to accomplish her assignment. She sets a timer to swap tasks.

This is how a youngster with a slow procession pace might develop and progress with the help and love and understanding of parents.

CHAPTER TWO

Why does my child act up?

"Children learn more from what you ARE than what you TEACH"

Whenever I heard the words 'act up' or' misbehave,' an event occurred in my mind. It was my daughter's sixth birthday, and we had thrown a party for friends, colleagues, and my spouse's boss, who arrived with his wife. We unexpectedly heard a young kid, screaming no you cannot play with us 'you are a doggie' and he was repeating this statement to the boss who was attempting to engage with these tiny tots while they were playing. Even though the boss handled the situation in a very entreating manner, this scenario was humiliating for the guardians, and they ended up yelling at the tiny child, who was oblivious of his poor behaviour. But who was to blame for the child's misbehaviour?

Where did the youngster get the word? These two questions remained unanswered and the little boy was punished for his conduct.

This is not the case with this couple, but it is with the majority of the parents. And made us wonder, "Why do children act badly?" Is the little boy to be labelled as bad or at fault?

One reason could be technological developments and the way society has revolutionised the style of living in the developing world, some of these changes have been extremely harmful to our children, and are increasingly harming adults as well.

Patterns have evolved all around the world, providing us with some information about children's changing behaviour. According to a study conducted by the American Academy of Paediatricians, the risk of mental instability and behavioural problems in children would increase by 50% globally.

Sometimes children have bad days. For several cases, children may exhibit less-than-ideal conduct. Perhaps they are exhausted, dissatisfied, or annoyed. Perhaps they've overindulged in sugar or are fatigued following an especially long day at school.

But what if bad days become more common, and unpleasant habits become a serious pattern?

A pattern of misbehaviour or "acting out" might indicate that the issue is more serious than a bad day. Many individuals mistakenly believe that repeating bad behaviour in their children signals that stronger discipline is required. Instead, children acting out can be a warning sign that something is wrong and that they cannot communicate their concerns orally.

Children are not born with the capacity to communicate their feelings. Instep, when things get unpleasant, chafing, and terrifying. Kids may express their sentiments by tossing of fit, ignoring headings. or denying to comply. On the off chance that those undesired sentiments go undetected and untreated, they can lead to the propensity of troublesome - and regularly perilous behaviour

To get it why do the kids, 'ACT OUT' it is imperative to understand 'ACT OUT'

What Exactly Is Acting Out?

Although most people understand what "act out" means, it is vital to describe it before considering possible causes.

Acting out often refers to bad behaviour that is physically hostile, harmful to property, verbally abusive, or otherwise more intense than basic misbehaviour. Act out has been characterized by the American Psychological Association as an intense behavioural display of emotions that releases stress or conveys these feelings in a veiled or indirect manner. Other terms used to characterise this conduct include aggression, defiance, disruptive behaviour, meltdowns, oppositional behaviour, and temper tantrums.

We frequently use the phrase "acting out" to describe activities that parents do not approve of. Acting out behaviours are detrimental to the family's day-to-day functioning. Some acting out behaviours are to be expected during the developmental phase of a youngster. As children become more independent and create their identities, they may push some limits and rebel against parental control. This allows students to put their individuality to the test in a comfortable environment. Children and teenagers may also misbehave to convey difficult-to-articulate thoughts, feelings, or experiences.

Indeed, whereas acting out is common conduct, it shows up diverse for each child and is decided by their improvement, identity, and capacity to manage stress or excruciating feelings. As the case may be, all exercises, indeed misbehaviours, have a reason. Children will act out to realize an objective or meet a requirement, even in the case, they are ignorant of what they desire.

A youth who does not need to clean his room, for illustration, may toss a fit. His guardians may at that point get distracted with alleviating him down and disregarding his assignments, in this way strengthening his upheaval. The youth learn that tossing fits get him out of doing things he doesn't want to do, and he may act so also within the future to maintain a strategic distance from other obligations.

Subsequently, when kids or youths fight, yell, hurl fits, get powerful, these hones are insinuated as acting out. It is exceptionally imperative to induce the cause of this conduct, whether it could be a youthful kid or an adolescent.

Signs of Extreme Behaviour

Any misbehaviour that has a substantial influence on a child's life and lasts for several months may indicate a problem. For example, if a youngster is enduring high amounts of stress at home, they may have recurrent outbursts to cope with the overwhelming sensations. Such actions may necessitate the assistance of a professional to diagnose the problem and treat the specific requirements of the family.

Overall, if a youngster behaves out for reasons other than normal development, the following can be the indicators:

- The misconduct interferes with school or a child's day-to-day functioning.
- The misbehaviour interferes with a parent's employment or ability to operate at home.
- The misbehaviour has an impact on the child's capacity to form and maintain good connections.
- Self-harming or suicidal threats, thoughts, or gestures are part of the activity.
- Typical parenting practices are no longer effective in changing behaviour.

Sometimes, it can be difficult for parents to adequately identify the reason and treat the problem when behaviours have complicated underlying concerns. Similarly, parents may be unaware that their child has a mental health problem.

Anxiety and despair can contribute to behavioural difficulties in many youngsters. According to the Centres for Disease Control and Prevention, approximately one in every three children aged 3 to 17 who have behaviour difficulties also has anxiety, and approximately one in every five has depression.

A kid or adolescent frequently lacks the self-awareness to articulate the cause for their misbehaviour, making it difficult to diagnose the problem. Parents, on the other hand, are not alone if their child is acting in ways they don't understand or can't manage to modify.

It is not always simple to pinpoint the causes of misbehaviour, as a variety of variables might have an impact on a kid. A mental health expert can assist a family in determining what is wrong and develop a treatment plan to teach coping skills.

Hillside, for example, employs dialectical behaviour therapy to assist children and families in developing a deeper awareness of problematic behaviours and replacing ineffective coping mechanisms with effective ones.

Why Is My Child Acting Out?

"Why do children act out?" is one of the most prevalent queries I've heard as an educator.

Many parents question whether they're doing anything wrong if they're not doing enough, and a variety of other emotions such as remorse and failure.

I should mention that every child acts out now and then. Acting out might appear different in various kids, but it usually involves challenging actions such as punching, sobbing, yelling, throwing or smashing objects, not listening, or saying NO to everything you say.

Why children behave out might be difficult to understand at first, but I can assure you that it is not your fault. There are several reasons why children act out, some of which are just a natural part of childhood development, while others may indicate something more serious.

At times, the exceptional act of a fit is implied to cover up the source of the bad content from parents. You will be astounded to memorise the fundamental cause of your child's bad conduct or fits.

Here are a few conceivable reasons why a child may be acting out.

Poor Parenting

- Improper Childcare

According to Anne-Marie Conn, a researcher at the University of Rochester Medical Center, the discoveries suggests that destitute child-rearing is passed down from era to era, like beating and shouting. Almost every parent aims to be a great parent. A few even though, never very cut. The working of both guardians has extended significantly over the world, taking off a tremendous void within the family. As a result of this move. kids spend a disturbing Sum of time alone subordinate on advances such as computers, and versatile phones for company. This has driven an increment in hurried and deceptive conduct among children.

- Intimidation to Discipline

"Parents who had a history of adversity were more prone to value physical punishment,"

Discipline means to instruct. It does not imply punishment. Punishment is not the sole method to educate. Punishment as the primary disciplinary tool is a sign of laziness in parenting. Because it is easier to halt undesirable conduct at the moment, some parents employ punishment indiscriminately. Punishment as a form of discipline teaches a child nothing. The youngsters have a punishing or aggressive stance. They learn that aggressiveness is an appropriate problem-solving strategy.

- Individual intrigued of parents

A few Guardians underscore their interface over the leading interface of the child. They need their children to fair comply with what they say. They intervene in subject choice, career or work alter. Residential savagery, physical savagery, sexual manhandling, or extreme discipline of a kid are all awful parenting features that contribute to undesirable conduct within the child.

Parents' Desire/Parental Pressure to Choose a Career

Choosing a job only to meet the expectations of one's parents is the most typical mistake made by students at a young age, which they later come to regret. Most kids from business families are encouraged to select commerce, and hence B.Com or BBA as their preferred career path. Some who fight succumb to family pressure, resulting in an unsatisfactory career graph. Such influences, disguised as following their guardians' wishes, are deemed unproductive for the pupils in the long term, and they may experience discomfort, disinterest, dull and irritated which leads to arrogance and disrespectful behaviour.

Disorders- Mental, Physical & Sensory Issues

i. A few children 'act out' because of untreated disorders. A few conditions which may be the root of the conduct, incorporate attention deficit hyperactivity disorder (ADHD), anxiety disorders, autism, and obsessive-compulsive disorder. While all of these letters can be widely treated with a combination of therapies. The treatment must moreover be befitting and steady.
ii. In a few cases children 'act out' because of unrecognised, tangible issues, such as sensory processing disorder, that may be unrecognised. For illustrations. Numerous children with autism may have sensory challenges that make conventional sights and sound physically painful. Many guardians have no clue that they have a child who needs additional care and consideration from experts.
iii. Another cause for 'acting out' is perhaps disappointment due to undiscovered or untreated learning incapacities. For example, dyslexia. Having untreated learning incapacities will result in long term troublesome conduct as your child comes up short to urge the assistance they got to learn correctly. This will result in advance troublesome conduct as they will fault themselves for not being able to concentrate or focus in class.

iv. An oppositional disobedient disorder (ODD) may be short of conduct disorder. It is generally analysed in childhood. Children with ODD are uncooperative, rebellious and unfriendly towards peers, guardians' instructors and specialist figures. They are more alarming to others than they are to themselves.

Other Factors

- Attaining attention

If youngsters do not accept, they are receiving the positive attention they require from a parent educator or another professional figure. They will acknowledge negative concentration. A child may feel they don't have a place unless another take note of them. In this way, a kid who feels ignored may or may not have a parent yell at them, causing them to feel overlooked. If a parent becomes upset by a kid's contact, the youngster is probably acting out for attention.

- Possessing Power

Children have little influence over the circumstances or situations wherein they find themselves. They don't get to pick whether or not to go to school, and they have no say. Acting out allows youngsters to feel in control when they would otherwise feel powerless.

A young kid may seek authority through a tantrum or ignoring a parent's order. As the kid grows older, he or she could become even more determined to take control of their life by engaging in damaging habits or defying parental requests. When a kid craves authority, a parent may feel challenged and the urge to exert control over the youngster.

- To exact vengeance

If children are unable to achieve authority or attention, they may attempt retaliation against one or both parents as a form of punishment. The youngster may believe they are unwanted and that they only belong if they can cause others to suffer the same anguish they are experiencing. They may say nasty words or cause damage to a family member's goods to punish them. Children who desire vengeance may lead their parents to be upset or horrified by their actions' exact vengeance

- To Demonstrate Inadequacy

A kid may exhibit inadequacy if they feel they are unable to accomplish one of the aforementioned aims or if they believe they are unable to match their parents' expectations. Children who believe they are inadequate may refuse to participate in an activity or finish a task. They may be reluctant to interact with others and may retreat from certain settings. If a parent is at a loss for what to do for their child and is anxious for a solution, the youngster is most likely hiding behind a veil of inadequacy.

Some more typical causes of children misbehaviour include:

- They are weary or hungry;
- They are afraid or frightened
- They are sad, irritated, or angry.
- An abrupt shift in routine
- Being irritated by sensory input such as loud noises or scratchy clothing

Putting their independence, a limit, or a boundary to the test

- In the past, it got them what they wanted.
- Stress caused by major life changes (for example, relocating, a new sibling, or a pandemic!)

Conclusion

Behaviour communicates. With this knowledge, we can shift the inquiry from "Why do children act out?" to "What is my child trying to tell me?"

Every acting out activity is motivated by a feeling or a desire. Knowing that this is the reason why youngsters act out, we can begin by understanding and meeting that need. We can then teach them healthier, more polite methods to communicate their feelings, wishes, and needs.

CHAPTER THREE

How to deal with Slow Processing Speed?

Let your child grow at their own pace

We live in a world that's fast-paced and oftentimes competitive. When it comes to our kids it is important to empower children to succeed, it is additionally critical to creating beyond any doubt that they're succeeding at their pace. That's the reason grades are disposed of within the instruction framework to let understudies work in a more competency-based framework. It is fundamentally critical to let youthful children pick up abilities at their pace for them to succeed.

Children are altered to memorize and develop up at a suitable pace. A parent's work, says the American Foundation of Paediatrics (AAP), is to sustain, energize and give an invigorating environment. Forget almost what kin did at the same age. Children are like fingerprints—no two are the same.

If you are aware that your child has a sluggish processing speed, you must make appropriate modifications. You should set your clock earlier than normal so that you can keep your youngster on track to accomplish his duties on time because they may appear to be sluggish or uninterested. In truth, they are working quite hard to stay up and simply want further assistance. They cannot just "be faster" since they cannot digest information as rapidly.

Most often it's a struggle that for my child completing homework is forever.

A ten-minute task takes thirty minutes. A twenty-minute task might take an hour. It isn't a lack of effort, a failure to comprehend the material, or a reluctance to attempt. Every night while doing schoolwork, I see my kid struggling to stay focused. We sit side by side at the table while I assist him in staying on track, yet it still takes longer.

Children are like wipes in that they come in a package. They splatter info and quickly learn considerably more data in a shorter period than any adult can manage. This does not imply that the youngster is harsh because he or she has no boundaries. Children, like everyone else, require time to assimilate information to apply it to real-life situations. It is vital to allow young children to develop competencies at their own pace to avoid discontent and to promote personalised learning.

My friend's kid began walking when she was only 9 months old, and my friend was overjoyed to watch her strolling all around the home. She began talking, however, at the age of three, due to a speech impediment. After a few rounds of therapy, she was able to talk fluently. She is presently a radio host and anchor for a variety of programmes. This illustrates that children think, learn, and grow distinctly.

It is required that parents must maintain reasonable expectations for their children. A 5-year-old, for example, will comprehend fundamental arithmetic abilities such as addition and subtraction and will be able to execute multiplication and division at a particular age.

-

Make your child conscious of one's individuality

Every youngster is unique in his or her skills; what counts is how much we can nurture them. Allow youngsters to grow and learn at their own pace. Different IQ levels are bestowed on children. Some of them are intellectually strong, while others have a talent for languages, and yet others are inventive, creative, and so on. It is unfair to expect a creative thinker to be rational and vice versa. We need to allow kids the freedom to be themselves.

Parents must teach their children that each of us has four to five distinct qualities and gifts. Almighty made each of us unique individuals, just as no two crystals are alike. Make children aware of the wonders of variety. We all have a life purpose, and no one else can finish or execute the task that you are particularly prepared for in life.

As parents, foster in your children a sense of awe-inspiring life and assist them in identifying their unique talents. Parents must encourage the child's strengths and talents, as well as their individual goals. Instil confidence in them, celebrate their successes, and congratulate them with encouraging words.

-

Accept, Understand and love unconditionally

Remember my cousin's story, which I recounted in the first chapter? My cousin chose to see a doctor about her daughter's behaviour since shouting all the time isn't helping either of them. The doctor verified that his daughter had 'Slow Procession Disorder.' The parent's perspective toward their child shifted as soon as they become aware of that fact and the hardship their daughter was suffering. Her parents embraced her as she is and encouraged her to perform her responsibilities at her own pace. Instead of shouting and screaming, they began calming and motivating her. My cousin and his daughter are now working together on the development plans recommended by the doctor, which has not only helped her develop but has also instilled confidence in her. They not only embraced their daughter's unique features but also showered her with unconditional love and helped her grow as a person.

The above instance illustrates that if you accept the children as they are and nurture them with unconditional love the child will blossom like a beautiful rose flower though sounded by thorns that still have the can mesmerise the people with its beauty and fragrance.

No doubt, it's tough to accept and empathise with the child who struggles to match the things on our timeline. We are well aware that Life is full of tasks that must be completed promptly, such as homework, housework, and getting to school on time. Your youngster will need to learn to advocate and flourish themselves. To flourish in today's environment, he will need to learn how to be more efficient.

However, with the correct atmosphere and genuine acceptance, our children may come up with unique and significant answers to challenges. They can teach us how to slow down and be more purposeful in our lives.

Parents must embrace, adore, and show affection for children, whenever they make mistakes or fall short of perfection.

When parents genuinely love their children, it leads to positive consequences such as improved brain development, the ability to build healthy connections, more stress tolerance, and a stronger immune system. Unconditional love instils confidence, fortitude to accept one's imperfections, and motivates children to work on growth goals.

Strategies do deal with Slow Processing Speed

- ### *Aware your child about slow processing speed*

Many parents are concerned that discussing or "identifying" their child's learning and cognitive difficulties would make him feel worse. However, consider that it might be difficult for children to grasp why it takes them so long to complete a test or answer a question. Knowing there is a reason—and a name—for their difficulties is reassuring to children and discussing it may be stimulating.

Help your youngster see things from a fresh perspective and explain that everyone has certain talents and limits.

Inform your child that processing speed has nothing to do with intelligence or "laziness." Many intelligent people have slower processing speeds.

Make your child understand that he is doing his best, but that his slow processing speed will affect him at school, at home, and in social situations, and that we will endeavour to improve it.

- ### *Understanding within all members of the family*

All members of the family must be aware of the slow processing speed to avoid taunting by siblings. To offset this, explain to the other youngsters that everyone learns differently and at a different rate.

Change the tempo, tone, and complexity of your communication with your children.

Become cautious (particularly if you're a parent with a rapid processing speed) of providing too much information too quickly.

Use both verbal and visual channels to help youngsters comprehend knowledge more quickly

- ### *Make some Room*

Children with different cognitive speeds may require more time to comprehend information. Don't overload your youngster, and allow him time to ask questions. Making time to listen to your child's feelings about what you've told him and how he feels might be beneficial.

Also, explain additional learning or cognitive impairments to your child if he or she suffers in those other areas. However, it is equally important to remind him that there are solutions available to help him with any problems he may be facing.

- ### *Create Routine*

Parents may help by providing more structure by using timetables, timings, clocks, alarms, and rewards. Establish a defined pattern and timetable to boost the speed; the more automatic or routine something is, the more likely it is to be finished effectively. It may be advantageous to involve older children in the problem-solving process. Enhance your child's awareness of time and help him or her with time management. Parents should refrain from personalising, punishing, or reacting emotionally, as slow processing speed is not purposeful and may be addressed.

- ### *Develop skills through practice*

Regular practise can help the child's talents to improve. Repeating a task, according to the study, makes it more automatic—and hence faster to process. This holds for tasks ranging from brushing your teeth to memorising multiplication tables. The more they practice a task, the quicker they will become at it.

- ***Enhance organisational and planning abilities.***

Planning may be challenging for certain kids due to their slow cognitive speed. Keeping a log of start and stop times may help with this process. Estimating how long a work will take and then tracking whether or not enough time was allotted may also be useful.

It may also help the child to be more efficient in everyday tasks. By sticking to routines, your child will have less new information to process.

- ***Stay Positive***

The slow processing speed may reduce as the child grows. Maximize child potential by keeping the expectation realistic. It will help to accommodate your child's need

- ***Speak with your child's school***

Check to see whether the child is eligible for classroom modifications due to his slow processing speed. It will give flexibility for more time to complete activities, such as taking an exam, which might help children feel less anxious as they work.

- Look into computer tools that can help you enhance your processing speed, such as Cogmed (www.cogmed.com), Captain's Log (www.braintrain.com), or Interactive Metronome (www.interactivemetronome.com).

Let your child spread their wings

It is very important to let the child set free to choose his/her path

When you give your child wings, they can learn at a much deeper level. Parents who are afraid of their child's sadness tend to prune their child's wings. You inadvertently prevent your child from participating in the journey that God has prepared for you. You should let them go as parents. Show your trust and blessings to them as you give them wings. "I know you can do it," you demonstrate to them. "You have my full confidence."

To nurture children in such a manner that they have a strong sense of self and belonging, while also instilling in them the confidence to fully stretch their wings & soar through unconditional love, trust, and respect.

Giving our children wings means allowing them to flee the nest. To have entire faith in their abilities and potential and show affection and care. If parents know their children, they can assist them in choosing the best professional decisions.

Know Your Child

Do not botch yourself into considering that being along with your child compares to knowing your child. Since the association you have got — or do not have — along with your children implies everything, it's time to begin developing it. It's straightforward to bond with a newborn, but a child is greater and sassier, it's more troublesome to keep that feeling alive. Despite this, it is the foremost imperative perspective of childhood. Life is, undoubtedly, frenzied. Your child will be a grown-up within the squint of an eye. Do not permit this invaluable fellowship to elude past your fingers. Take the time to urge to know her on a more profound level and to appreciate her unmistakable highlights.

Therefore, to understand the potential of the child it is important to know your child in-depth.

Let's be true to ourselves and take a self-test on how much you know your Kids?

1. What are your child's shortcomings according to you? list Them.
2. List your child's passion?
3. Are you aware of your child's talents?
4. Are you aware of what makes your child happy?
5. Are you aware of what he/she enjoys doing?
6. Are you aware of what your kid aspires to become in life?

7. Do you know what's causes the child to be irritated and angry at times?
8. Are you available to speak to him at any time?
9. Are you the best pal for your child?
10. Is your child free to say anything without fear or hesitation?

If the majority of the questions are answered negatively, it is necessary to take a pause and speak with your kid to get answers to all of your questions. You will learn about your child's goals and where they are stuck.

Understanding Potential

"Everyone is a genius. But if you judge a fish by its ability to climb a tree, it will live its whole life believing that it is stupid."

Albert Einstein.

Every child is a genius, unique and wonderful. God has endowed each person with a unique set of abilities and potential, which they may use to shine and thrive. Every child is uniquely gifted, and no two children can or should be compared. They each have their distinct personality.

"Potential is an unseen unknown that cannot be measured."

Most of the time, parents fail to identify their children's strengths and force them to do something that is not their strong suit. As parents, we are concerned about the well-being of our children. We want the best for our children and want them to be successful and happy in life. In our anxiety, we tend to drive children into a rat race and fail to acknowledge their genuine potential.

Parents need to provide supports and buffers, and also to be there to listen, advise, affirm, and soothe their children as they navigate the ups and downs of daily life—and NOT to make assumptions about prospective problems.

Many parents have a highly rigid view of life, believing that a person is fortunate mainly if they have a typical career, such as a doctor, engineer, banker, or teacher.

They are unable to comprehend that there are plenty of other areas in which their child may succeed and be the greatest. We should accept our child's distinctiveness and appreciate their strengths to help them be happy and successful.

Children are full of promise, and when given the correct opportunity, they become successful and happy whatever they are doing into beautiful persons. Parents must acknowledge and foster their children's talents, allowing them to attain their greatest potential.

Let us assist children in enjoying and learning from everything that life has to offer, rather than calling into doubt their intelligence, creativity, self-confidence, or excitement by discussing or concentrating on their potential.

Recognizing the Potentials of Children with Slow Processing Speed

Parents frequently express anxiety that their children with poor processing speeds may be unable to complete their schooling or obtain a meaningful profession owing to the fast-changing and extremely demanding demands in the workplace. While speed is important in many areas of study and employment, it is simple to see that many children with poor processing speed have attributes that make them a good fit for certain sorts of jobs when we take a step back and think about it.

Parents and instructors must assist children with slow processing speed in identifying their strengths, particularly those that are unaffected by slow processing speed. Perhaps a youngster is particularly creative or artistic, with a passion for design, data analysis, research, or service to others. Children with slow processing speeds might thrive in activities that require them to listen and get to know others. They also do well in situations when attention to detail is more crucial than speed.

Consult Career coach/counsellor for right career choice

Career counselling is a service that assists people in determining the best career route for them. Career counsellors, often known as "career coaches" or "job coaches," offer advice providing direction and alternative career pathways to professionals of various industries, backgrounds, and experiences.

Clients of a career counsellor may seek advice on their current job hunt, insight into a mid-career industry move, or general professional development help. It is the job of the career counsellor to assist you in understanding your alternatives and evaluating difficult professional decisions.

Career counsellors also help individuals by giving information, administering examinations, and advising them on how to land a fantastic job.

Parents must talk with and encourage their children to seek career advice from career coaches. Career coaches take the help of a psychometric tool that create detailed and personalised report catering to 5 dimensions: Oriental style, interests, personality, aptitude, and emotional quotient.

Experience of a mother ...

Helen a proud mother of a slow processor discussed desirable characteristics and prospective jobs that her daughter may pursue, which could be encouraging for many youngsters with slow processing speeds.

My daughter's processing speed is sluggish, although she excels in many things. She's a terrific musician, so a music career would be ideal for her. She may be a composer or a music therapist; she has no fear of performing since she is self-assured. She could even offer pre-recorded YouTube lessons. If it's not alive, she can take as much time as she wants. Because they aren't live and can be practised and planned, many social media positions might work.

ART, DOMESTIC SCIENCE, CAKE DECORATING, INVENTOR ARTS AND CRAFTS are some of her other skills. TAYLOR, JEWELLER, BEAUTICIAN, REFLOXOLOGIST, NATURAL THERAPIST, DESIGNER, SPORTS CAREER She excels at abseiling, swimming, and skiing!! DANCING!! She has the potential to be a dancer or a photographer. There are a lot!!

Her short-term memory is bad, but it improves when it comes to money!! So far, she has raised funds for Barbados and cancer research. Her difficulties have made her a highly determined person!!!

It demonstrates that with support, love and positivity children can overcome any obstacles.

CHAPTER FOUR

How to deal with Child's behaviour?

"In my world, there are No Bad Kids, just impressionable, conflicted young people wrestling with emotions &impulses, trying to communicate their feelings & needs the only way they know how." Janel Lansbury

In the second chapter, we discussed why children act out and listed the causes for their behaviour. In this chapter, we'll look at how to rock-bottom with a misbehaving youngster. Before we get into how to deal with a misbehaving child, it's essential to understand what we shouldn't do as a parent. A parent should avoid yelling and name-calling.

It is often seen when children misbehave, we as parent's try to control the situation by hook or crook method. Though these reactions may prevent a kid from doing what they are doing at the time, they have no long-term or lasting good influence and do not teach the child to possess socially acceptable behaviour in the society

Furthermore, these emotions hurt the parent-child connection and can affect your child's self-esteem, confidence, and regular social development.

Children learn by example, so if you yell at or strike your youngster, you're teaching him that yelling and hitting are affirmative behaviour. Therefore, it is preferable to lead by good examples.

So, rather than punishing, we must discipline!

Disciplining children, especially stubborn kids, is a daunting task for parents. But it makes the children aware of the appropriate and undesirable conduct, it also teaches them how to react to challenging situations as adults. If you respond to misbehaviour with rational discussion and problem solving, your children will learn to do the same.

•

Ways to rock bottom misbehaviour

So, when your kid misbehaves

1.
Remain calm. Take time to respond and not react

To induce unbending of the circumstance to turn worst. It is all right to step away from a circumstance and donate time to cool off. Conceding discipline gives you time to mull over sensible disciplinary activity and time for your child to think approximately what they have done. Be clear simply need time to calm down, which you may examine the matter after you are prepared. Avoid labelling your child as "obstinate," "naughty," or "bad," since this will have an impact on their behaviour.

2. Determine the cause of conduct

Determine the cause of the misconduct by posing the right questions "Do you feel tired?" "Do you need me?" "Is it too noisy in here?" "Do you need something?" and so on. This not only shows them that you sympathise, understand, and appreciate them, but it also shows that you are eager to investigate their requirements. The objective is for them to calm down with these sorts of articulations because when a child is crying and throwing a tantrum, they are not within the outline of intellect to require any frame of critique.

3.
Provide a solution

Depending on the circumstances, this can be accomplished in a variety of ways. Provide choices if they are not tuned in or being insistent. For example, "do you need to finish your schoolwork now or in 10 minutes?" or gain a "Yes" from them, "would you want to go to the park...?" Okay, let's finish our food soon." If they are being sneaky, ask for their assistance, shift their attention to something else, or remind them of their limitations and the penalties that have already been stated. If they're throwing a temper tantrum, tell them you'll convert to them when they're calm.

4.

Reward them for their positive behaviour

Recognize and reward your child for their good behaviour. Attempt to dodge material rewards and focus on nonmaterial rewards such as playing an amusement with them, taking them to their favourite place or permitting them to remain up 15 minutes past their bedtime or 5 mins more screen time. What I want to convey is parenting should not be a struggle, it should be fun seeing them grow, feeling confident when they overcome their struggles. Parents when teaching their children patience and love they can make them feel safe loved, and valued. The way parent treat/deal with their children during their worst time have positive reinforcement and it is far more effective than punishment.

5.

Let children learn from Natural Consequences

In the olden days, during our time discipline simply means losing privileges for bad behaviour. No homework, no television for a week. Recent research suggests that it is not the ideal way to teach life skills. When you allow your child to learn via natural consequences, he or she is more likely to grasp the implications of their actions. Therefore, many experts advise parents to let their children experience what they refer to as "the natural repercussions of their behaviour". For example, if your child refuses to eat allow them to starve—they won't fight next time.

6.

Be Steady

In any case of the discipline, you select for your child, you must be reliable each time they lock in undesirable conduct. Kids are discerning, and they will choose up on anything blemishes you have got. Kids will take advantage of a feeble parent who does not take after through on their "threats" and will proceed to lock in the undesirable conduct.

7.

Utilize the time-out approach for wanted conduct

The time-out strategy works well with little children. Clarify to the understudies what a time out is. When the undesirable conduct happens, advise the kid that it is unsatisfactory and caution him or her that if the conduct does not terminate, he or she will be put in time-out. Stay cool and dodge looking incensed, and if getting out of hand continues, discreetly expel him or her to the time-out region. Rather than examining the negative conduct, look for strategies to laud and empower positive conduct afterwards on.

8.

Be Realistic with Your Expectations

One of the most important factors to remember while bringing up the child is to keep our expectations realistic. Children are bound to make mistakes at some point in time, and a parent needs to deal with them. As parents, you have to realize the potential and capability of your child. It is wrong to keep high expectations from children. The unrealistic expectations exceed the potential that the child has, it can be harmful to the child's development and self-image. So, parents need to be patient for the child's skills and interests to develop in his formative years.

9.

Set Strong Ground Rules

As a parent, you need to set down rules for your kid, especially after he has started school. Make a routine timetable for a kid. Set out fixed hours for playtime, homework and screen time. Give him 15 minutes every day to clean his room and an hour to relax out in the garden. Try to make a flexible routine and don"t be too strict while allocating time for study and play. Keeping adequate time for playing sports help in both physical and mental development.

10.

Practice to make intension of the Day

Intension helps to focus on a moment. Daily intentions can help to complete a particular task in the set time frame. They also provide a roadmap and reminder for how to live out each day. Intentions give you purpose, as well as the inspiration and motivation to achieve your purpose. The practice of setting daily intentions can change your life.

11.

Teach Accountability

After a certain period, every parent expects their children to be accountable and responsible. When parents act as role models for their children, it makes it easier for them to learn and be accountable. Because children learn best via observation, parents must hold themselves accountable at home daily. This might be accomplished by developing a set of rules to follow.

Each member of the household, for example, can be allocated a certain responsibility for each day of the week. Then, guarantee that parents are always capable of sticking to the specified guidelines. If you don't, explain your mistake and promise to do better the next time.

Your children will rapidly recognise the importance of accountability and will be less hesitant to apologise for their mistakes.

Conclusion

Therefore, no child is bad and no behaviour is wrong. There is always a story behind every behaviour. As a parent, we need to think of different methods to fix the behaviour in the right direction.

Great Imitators Observing – Be cautious

Children are great imitators. So, give them something great to imitate.

"Parents are the first instructors and role models for their children."

They are in charge of moulding the child's conduct and instilling positive ideals in them. Children observe, mimic, and listen to their parents. As a result, they must serve as positive role models for the children. To expect their child to follow their lead, parents must do what they teach. However, the vast majority of parents fail horribly in this regard, instead of setting negative models of parenting.

Parenting is with no doubt one of the toughest and demanding responsibilities in the world. To be a successful parent, you must constantly learn and make sacrifices. To raise well-behaved and responsible children, one must be ready to commit significant time, patience, and energy. Instilling and inculcating positive values in a youngster will result in him or her being a decent person in the future.

Children learn through their environment, but "Parents are a child's first instructors and role models." They are in charge of regulating the child's conduct and instilling positive ideals in them. Children observe, mimic, and listen to their parents. As a result, they must serve as positive role models for the children. Many newborns, for example, mimic facial motions like putting out their tongues. Children are excellent mimics. As a result, we must be cautious about what kids hear and see around them for them to emulate what is proper.

Before saying anything in front of the child, guardians ought to consider the effect it may have on their child's intellect and future. Keep in mind the occurrence between a small child and my husband's boss? Children learn more through witnessing, hence we must be cautious in our practices. We may educate kids on compassion through helping others, making a kind gesture, or appreciating money.

Parents should set a good example for their children by washing their plates after lunch or dinner, or when they arrive home, they should keep their belongings in places, such as shoes in the shoe rack, keys in the key holder, and washing their hands and feet before sitting down for a cup of tea or coffee.

Children not only observe how we talk and act. It moreover relates to what individuals take note of around them. For illustration, consider movies and cartoons. Guardians must be watchful and mindful, and ought to prompt their children on worthy movies and cartoons. As a result, guardians must control what their children see and listen to. Children turn to us, grown-ups, for direction. Guardians may direct and motivate their children by demonstrating pictures of trust, administration, mettle, and equity using their activities.

To be a successful parent, you must constantly learn and make sacrifices. Instilling excellent values in a youngster will make him or her a better person and citizen in the future.

Live Child's Dream

On my campus, there was a 12-year-old fellow named 'Dhruv' who was obsessed with hockey and never missed an opportunity to play. His seniors regarded him for his ability, but his parents gave importance to scholastics over games, and sports were not considered a reasonable proficient choice. His guardians were restricted to his diversion and needed him to score well in school to guarantee him a successful 9-5 lucrative job in a tech company. His father chastened him anytime he caught him playing, but Dhruv decided to pursue to play his game in any case. When the father found out about the low score in the half-yearly exam, his temper rose and beat the child with the hockey stick that led to a fracture of his leg. Since then, the adolescent has never touched a hockey puck. He is as of now working for the railways, but despite a few openings, he has not been able to play once more. He's working, as winning is essential, but with no eagerness. His childhood scars still show today when he speaks about it to close friends. On the other hand, if his father would have encouraged him to follow his passion for hockey, he would have done something exceptional and would have been blissful in life.

Dreams bring a feeling of security in these volatile and uncertain times. However, our parents' expectations frequently become a load on our shoulders, and their ambitions become a responsibility. When it comes to job development, many Indian parents push their preferences on their children. While they want to raise their children to be physicians, scientists, and engineers, they unwittingly destroy their children's innocence and set them up for a lifetime of the rat race, with no disregard for their dreams and pleasure.

We must let our children be individuals, rather than extensions of ourselves. We must let our children pursue their aspirations, rather than expecting them to fulfil the dreams of their parents. Whether it is fulfilling our own unfulfilled goals or the new ones we begin weaving for our children once we become parents, it all comes down to making us proud or delighting us. But it's not about us; it's about THEM!

Most parents encourage their children to participate in activities that they like. Parents who enjoy reading, for example, may take their children to bookshops, whereas keen gardeners may enjoy spending time in the park.

Recently, my understudy approached me to induce clarity on stream choice. Both guardians are engineers and hence upset as their child pointed towards humanities. After the intro session, I proposed the parent take a psychometric evaluation to get clarity on his aptitude, interest, personality and orientation style. And based on it the detailed report paved the path for the right career choices in alignment with strength and potential. Guardians were a little distrustful around taking the test and informed me that they will get back. After two days when I called them to settle a date for the psychometric evaluation, to my shock mother said that he will not take the test as we both have persuaded him to acquire a science stream, as we both are engineers and we want our child to be an engineer.

Here, I want to emphasise that parents do affect their children's professional decisions, directly and indirectly.

The parent must remember that his or her major obligation is to be involved in their child's career management, coaching, commercial or emotional concerns, and so on. This might be a very good aspect of their connection; the option should be presented and agreed upon by their children so that the parameters of the parent-child relationship are honoured. When parents regard their children as business partners rather than sons and daughters, they are more likely to have "clients" rather than successful children.

In many respects, children vary from their guardians. Even though children share several interfaces and wish with their guardians, they will almost certainly have separated interfaces and ambitions. Trying to satisfy a need via your child is essentially detrimental since it ignores that child's individuality.

Pushing a youngster into a biased position may prevent the teenager from attaining their maximum potential and achieving their objectives.

CHAPTER FIVE

Words have great power; use them wisely

"Words have a magical power, they can either bring the greatest happiness or the deepest despair"

Sigmund Freud

Have you ever noticed that the more you limit your child from doing something, the more it comes back to you? This is due to the negative vibrations we produce in our minds through concepts and, eventually, the use of negative words such as Not...Don't.

Let's look at an example to see what I mean.

Assume you want your child to play flawlessly in a basketball game, and you continuously urge them not to make mistakes or drop the ball out from concern, and inevitably, the ball gets dropped. The reason for this is that your mind is always listening to the don't, and our minds have a hard time comprehending a negative image. To comprehend the don't drop instruction, the brain had to first image dropping, and then try and convince the brain not to do whatever it had just imagined.

Similarly, if you want to reinforce something, use the positive term what you desire rather than what you don't want. Because the mind cannot distinguish between good and negative thoughts, you will attract what you affirm. So, if you want your children to act appropriately, tell children what you expect, instead of what you need not intend them to do.

When I recognized the power of words, I have become more cautious in how I used them throughout the day. I changed my negative statements to positive ones and began focusing on what I wanted rather than what I didn't want.

We all know Words, may inflict deeper wounds than swords, and wounds inflicted by words take a long time to heal, and occasionally do not heal at all. That is something that almost all of us have heard. But how aware are we when we pick our words, especially when dealing with children? We are frequently unaware of, and often dismiss, the influence that bad comments may have on our children.

Positive words, according to Andrew Newberg, M.D. and Mark Waldman, authors of Words May Change Your Brain, "can modify the expression of genes, strengthening regions in our frontal lobes and enhancing the brain's cognitive performance."

The research on the power of positive words is astounding. Parents may help their children grow a healthy brain by using more positive words at home.

When a person receives encouraging words and reassurance, they perform better at work, become happier, and have a greater sense of value and significance.

Consider the following...

How much better would people feel and act if positive and encouraging phrases were the norm rather than the typical everyday jargon of negativity?

Consider the following African tribe. Whenever anyone commits anything bad in this tribe, they take the offender to the middle of the village then circle the individual for two days, saying all the nice things the person has done in their life. The tribe thinks that everyone is nice, yet errors happen, which are true cries for help. They band together to reconnect with them and their good nature.

Isn't it beautiful? Regularly, we all should emulate this sort of behaviour towards friends and family.

Conclusion

Words have tremendous power. One encouraging phrase may transform someone's life. Words have the power to heal and uplift. Your words, when uttered truthfully, have the power to influence people's lives. Consider your communication style. Your words can inspire others to reach greatness. Your words may comfort and even heal someone who is in pain. Your words can nurture, nourish, and inspire your children.

It is crucial to acknowledge that the impact of encouraging words extends to grownups as well. Parents owe it to themselves to work with their internal voices, which frequently hear the negative more than the good. Finding opportunities to hear and using encouraging words improves the overall well-being of a family.

For example, how do you feel when someone calls you dumb, ignorant, and good for nothing... not good... right, and you begin to doubt yourself?

Imagine how you will feel if someone praises you and loves your effort; I am sure you will be filled with confidence. The same thing happens to that youthful mind: it begins to doubt itself.

Parent the child you have, not the child you would want to have

As soon as a child is born, we begin to fantasise about them, how they'll be like, as well as how successful children will be in life. You may have wished for your children to be passionate about sports or academics, but the reality sets in as soon as our child is uninterested in becoming a doctor or engineer. And accept the fact that our children are not what we wanted them to be.

This is a lesson that many of us must acquire while we raise our children. Accepting your kid is the foundation for setting, expressing, and enforcing acceptable behaviour standards. And it's how you'll learn to respond to him in the most meaningful and effective way.

As you let go of the idealized image of whom the child should have been and embrace them for who they are, you learn to enjoy them as a developing individual. Due to this understanding, a far deeper love may blossom

Accepting your children contributes to their being. If parents completely accept their children's likes and dislike, peculiarities, limits, and choices the children will develop a deep relationship which will be based on acceptance, feeling loved, and eventually being a responsible individual.

Children want their parents to accept, adore and show affection. If they make errors or fall short of expectations, they should grab their hands for guidance and tell them that they will with them no matter what happens. This is what unconditional love entails. In other words, it is love with no ties attached. As a result, parents should love their children for who they are, rather than what they desire them to be.

Conclusion

No two individuals are the same; we are all unique in some manner, such as our ideas, skin colour, physical appearance, and so on. We must all accept this variety. Parents should recognise their children's accomplishments and unconditionally embrace their children's differences.

Be Mindful- Respond before reacting

Have you ever heard of the amygdala? If so, you should be familiar with how the amygdala works. When our brain detects a threat, it sends a signal toward the amygdala, the body's "alert" system, which instructs our bodies to behave without thinking. The amygdala reacts to events by initiating a fight, flight, or freeze reaction. This is to protect us, but our stress receptors are incapable of distinguishing between actual and illusory hazards. In everyday parenting, our stress reaction is sometimes inappropriately aroused by circumstances that are not genuinely life-threatening. For example, if your child does anything wrong, we quickly get furious or shout at them.

Similarly, most of our lives are spent reacting to individuals and events around us, and as a result, they might make others unhappy, make things worse for ourselves, or worsen the situation.

We frequently 'React' without thinking. Responding, on the other hand, is taking in the circumstance and deciding on the best course of action based on values such as reason, compassion, collaboration, and so on.

Reaction

For example, consider the case of Dhruv, whose father grew enraged after receiving a poor score in his half-yearly examinations and severely assaulted him without hesitation, so damaging the relationship rather than improving it. As consequence, reacting to the situation without thinking or pausing worsens the problem.

Respond

Again, in the instance of Dhruv, when his father discovered his son's poor grades, he became enraged, but he paused, took a deep breath, and considered the issue. The first answer is to inquire how his academics are doing – is he having any difficulties, is he scared? Second, inquire as to the explanation for his poor grades and how he might improve. Third, assist him with time management and scheduling. Fourth, gently discuss the value of studies, allow him to show himself, and hug him.

There will always be external events that bother us, but if we learn to respond and not just react, we can make things better and not worse.

How to Learn to Respond

The most important thing to learn is mindfulness and pausing.

Mindfulness entails paying attention to oneself when something that might typically disturb or elicit an emotional reaction occurs.

Then take a breather. We don't have to act right away just because we have an internal reaction. We may halt, not act, and simply breathe. It indicates we should gracefully exit the problems and give ourselves time to calm down before responding.

Three essential aspects of mindful parenting

1. Recognize your sentiments while you're arguing with your child.
2. Learn to pause before responding angrily.
3. Pay close attention to a child's point of view, even if you disagree with it.

Conclusion

It may be challenging the first and second times, but with experience, you will become more adept at pausing.

Take note of what triggered your emotion and pay attention if something similar happens again. Pause for a moment to be mindful, and pause, to develop a meaningful, compassionate approach. Share your responses with youngsters by telling them your story.

Make your children responsible

Children should be made responsible from a very young age. Parents by making rules and by following themselves can teach their children accountability. At home, each person should be made responsible for some of the other work. And they need to perform their duties without reminding.

For example - A toddler can be trained to pick their toys after playing. They should be made responsible for keeping their things in place. Young children should be made responsible for cleaning their innerwear, Ironing, packing bags, completing assignments/homework etc. This brings a sense of responsibility in the children to take ownership of their conduct.

I remember, 12th class students of my school were always blamed for their misbehaviour but when we went for a school trip the way these elder students have taken responsibility for young ones and luggage was commendable.Children will take ownership if they get an opportunities

Conclusion

Recognize your flaws and demonstrate how you attempt to rectify the damage caused by your errors. Just as adults, it's indeed difficult to accept responsibility for our acts. By starting early and providing a secure environment for your kid to accept the consequences of his behaviour, you will be assisting him in maturing into a mature, responsible adult who has a beneficial effect on society.

Overview

The book "Accepting Children Unconditionally" is about children who have been subjected to yelling, name-calling, spanking, and shouting as a result of their slow processing speed and behaviour. Children with slow transaction speeds are mistakenly thought by their parents and teachers to be lazy, neglectful, and stubborn owing to ignorance.

Slow processing speed, according to the book, is related to a method of sending information to the brain and has nothing to do with intelligence.

The book demonstrates that every activity has a purpose, yet as adults, we ignore the signs of that behaviour. The book also discusses the causes of poor processing speed and Act Up.

The book discusses how to deal with poor processing speed and acting out.

The book's goal is to persuade parents of the importance of knowing their children. so that parents may collaborate with their children on expert-recommended development strategies.

Printed by Libri Plureos GmbH in Hamburg, Germany